BETTER *Me*

365 Ways to **Transform Your Every Day Life**

WAEL IBRAHIM

First published by Ultimate World Publishing 2019

Copyright © 2019 Wael Ibrahim

ISBN

Print: 978-1-925884-21-0

Ebook: 978-1-925884-22-7

Wael Ibrahim has asserted his right under the Copyright, Designs and Patents Act 1988 to be identified as the author of this work. The information in this book is based on the author's experiences and opinions. The publisher specifically disclaims responsibility for any adverse consequences, which may result from use of the information contained herein. Permission to use information has been sought by the author. Any breaches will be rectified in further editions of the book.

All rights reserved. No part of this publication may be reproduced, stored in or introduced into a retrieval system, or transmitted in any form, or by any means (electronic, mechanical, photocopying, recording or otherwise) without the prior written permission of the author. Any person who does any unauthorised act in relation to this publication may be liable to criminal prosecution and civil claims for damages. Enquiries should be made through the publisher.

Cover design: Ebony Harper

Editor: J. P. Bautista

Typeset and layout: Ultimate World Publishing

Ultimate World Publishing

Diamond Creek,

Victoria Australia 3089

www.writeabook.com.au

DEDICATION

BetterMe is dedicated to the best people in my life: my late Dad, Mum, wife, and all my gorgeous children: Fagr, Hams, Habiba, and Ibrahim.

This book is also dedicated to all those who have inspired me throughout the years: my mentors, teachers, those who admire my work and, of course, my precious students.

Thanking you all is not enough.

ABOUT THE AUTHOR

Wael Ibrahim is best known for his work on fighting the plague of pornography addiction and the harmful impacts of irresponsible media.

He's an international speaker, trainer, teacher and a certified life coach. He is also the founder of *MentorPLUS* and a very proud family man of an unmatched mother, siblings, great wife, and precious children. Currently, Wael lives in Australia as he works as a student counsellor in one of the largest schools in Western Australia

TABLE OF CONTENTS

TESTIMONIALS .... **VII**

LIFE ON THE RIGHT PATH WITH THE RIGHT ATTITUDE 1

HOW WE SHOULD TREAT EACH OTHER 107

BEING OF SERVICE TO OTHERS 151

FAMILY AND MARRIAGE 167

SUCCESS AND GREATNESS 197

TAKING ACTION 229

FOCUS, PASSION AND PERSEVERANCE 261

OVERCOMING ADVERSITY 285

ON LEADERSHIP 307

ON ADDICTION 323

KNOWLEDGE AND WISDOM 335

REFLECTING ON EVERYDAY LIFE 353

TESTIMONIALS

"*BetterMe 365 Ways* to Transform Your Everyday Life is a wonderful daily reflection book full of great wisdom. It contains quotes to improve your mindset, confidence, relationships and more. With space to write down your own thoughts, this book allows its readers truly to internalize each quote and apply wisdoms to their unique life circumstances. Every home needs this book – keep it by your bedside, read and discuss daily with family members, give it as a valuable gift to loved ones – Its uses and benefits are many. I sincerely congratulate Wael on producing such a resourceful book that will serve to remind us all about important essential core values and moral principles."

– Calisha Bennett
– Author and founder of Developing Diamonds.

"I love the concept that Wael Ibrahim has come up with to challenge our thinking and have us reflecting on daily bases. When you commit to this practice daily, truly slow down and think about it, reflect on what it means and then take pen to paper to write down your thoughts, there is an inevitable mindset shift. Try it, you'll see for yourself."

– **Kathryn Jones,
Emotional Resilience Coach,
Back to The Fitrah Coaching Academy.**

"*BetterMe 365 Ways to Transform Your Everyday Life* is a must-read to develop the right attitude toward life and to work toward the best version of yourself. It is your daily companion to inspire you – especially when life gets tough for you to then pour your reflections below.

I read this book at a time where I needed guidance, and strength, that to reflect on all 365 quotes selectively compiled from Wael's own mentors and talks was a source of direction and hope. I have no doubt that whenever you feel trapped in life, you will find your way out through these quotes. It is life having your very own personal mentors guide you in different areas of your life. It is your daily encouragement – a gift wrapped in quotes ready for you to take in and reflect."

– **Sa'diyya Nesar**
– **Author of Strength from Within**

Life on the Right Path with the Right Attitude

you wish to attain. They were uttered and recorded during the sincerest moments of my life, they've impacted thousands of people and they might just have the same positive impact on you. Do your best to embark on that journey on a daily basis, reflect on what you read, interpret them within your own context and situations, then note your reflections in the spaces provided for you after every quote.

BetterMe is not about ME. It is an interactive book between the minds of those who have brought about these words out of me, and you the reader, who could inspire thousands of more people too just by sharing your own reflections over what you've read with me.

Remember, reading on its own isn't a real skill, translating what you read into actionable reality is what makes reading truly beneficial. So, enjoy the journey of becoming a BetterYOU every day in your life.

Wael Ibrahim – 2019

INTRODUCTION

"A short saying oft contains much wisdom."
— *Sophocles*

Honestly, I was stuck to jot down my thoughts in order to come up with the right introduction. I asked my wife for ideas, she started talking about every subject in the world and as a result we both got very confused. I was not interested in any of her ideas and we were both laughing at each other. THEN . . . I decided to keep it simple.

Words can make us, break us, inspire us, hurt us, bring about tears, laughter, bring down nations and make other nations rise and prosper. Words are our own products, so we better be wise when presenting them, because not paying attention to what we say is what could literally destroy hearts.

BetterMe is focused on the positive aspect of words usage. The 365 ways or quotes that were compiled in this book are meant to shift your condition from the negative to the best version of positivity that

1 PRINCIPLES

"We can compromise many things,
but never values and principles."

Your own reflections go here:

2 GRATITUDE

"Appreciate the little things,
but believe you can do more."

Your own reflections go here:

3 WRONG IS WRONG

"There's no way around it. Wrong will always remain wrong, even if you think there's a 'right' approach around it."

Your own reflections go here:

4 BE YOU

"Don't let the masses define who you are;
be yourself, for we are all unique."

Your own reflections go here:

5 COMPLAIN NOT, IF YOU ARE NOT CONTRIBUTING

"You will never be rewarded in life unless you are contributing to society and the world at large."

Your own reflections go here:

6 SAY SORRY PROUDLY

"Only courageous people apologize when they realize they've made a mistake. Saying sorry is not a sign of weakness. It is a mark of bravery and honesty."

Your own reflections go here:

7 HONESTY TO ONE'S SELF

"Honesty is easier to come by when you are sitting alone. In solitude, it is clearer if your actions
were right or wrong. If you were wrong, make amends publicly and without fear."

Your own reflections go here:

8 ADMITTING MISTAKES

"When you realize that you have made an error, admitting it is the first step in achieving success on your next attempt."

Your own reflections go here:

9 CHANGE

"Never underestimate the power of change within you."

Your own reflections go here:

10 PATIENCE

"Endure your pain a bit longer than usual; that is patience."

Your own reflections go here:

11 PATIENCE, AGAIN

"The moment you say 'I've been patient for too long' reveals you never practiced patience in the first place."

Your own reflections go here:

12 THE BEST VERSION OF WHO YOU ARE

"Do not pretend to be someone else. Be yourself and excel to be the best version of who you truly are."

Your own reflections go here:

13 WE ARE ALL EQUAL

"To look down upon others is the greatest sign of arrogance. If you are there, forget about success."

Your own reflections go here:

14 TOXIC PEOPLE

"Negative people and their remarks will never cease to exist. They are there as your test.
Now your job in life is to prove them wrong."

Your own reflections go here:

15 LOVE YOURSELF

"Love yourself, not to the extent of becoming arrogant and selfish, but value yourself and that which you can do to serve humanity."

Your own reflections go here:

16 DO NOT QUIT

"Just keep doing your best. Quitting is not for those who envision their success every single day of their lives."

Your own reflections go here:

17 HAPPINESS IS NOT A GOAL

"Do not run after happiness. Happiness results from doing what you love the most. It should not be a goal."

Your own reflections go here:

18 TRIVIAL ISSUES SHOULD NOT BOTHER YOU

"You've been given a good spouse, a decent job, gorgeous children, a decent home, all of which are NOT perfect, so do not think too much of the trivial issues that bother you. Rather, focus on the blessings associated with your spouse, job, children, and home."

Your own reflections go here:

19 APPRECIATION

"Appreciate what you have now. Don't be after what others possess; this is a recipe for unhappiness and discontent."

Your own reflections go here:

20 SELFLESSNESS

"We need you. The world needs you. Yes, YOU and everyone else. So, do not be selfish, and share what you know."

Your own reflections go here:

21 TRUTHFULNESS

"Let it be your best policy in life, speaking the truth."

Your own reflections go here:

22 ELSIE TU

I asked Elsie Tu of Hong Kong, "How come you are still working?" The 100-year-old lady answered with no hesitation, "If I stop working, I die."
(Elsie Tue had passed away at the age of 102 in the year 2015)

Your own reflections go here:

23 ENVY

"Envy is yet another key to failure and unhappiness."

Your own reflections go here:

24 CONTENTMENT

"Contentment is all you need to create a happy life. Find it within yourself."

Your own reflections go here:

25 THE TONGUE

"Use the tongue wisely. It could make you or break you. It could, in fact, break up families and nations; so, keep it still when needed."

Your own reflections go here:

26 DON'T BE DOUBLE-FACED

"Don't you agree that double-faced people are the most hated and despised by others? Well, don't be one of them."

Your own reflections go here:

27 SPEAK ONLY WHEN NECESSARY

"Don't speak just because you believe you must say something. Speak only when necessary, only when you can add value and change hearts."

Your own reflections go here:

28 LEARN TO SHARE

"It is hard to keep your thoughts and words only to yourself. It is mentally torturing. Learn to share what you feel and you shall be heard."

Your own reflections go here:

29 CONTENTMENT AGAIN

"Life may seem unfair to some; but trust me, if you are content, then life would appear to be more than fair."

Your own reflections go here:

30 IT IS OK TO SAY NO

"In an age of distraction from what is necessary, it is essential for you to learn to say NO to that which does not benefit you or does not align with your values."

Your own reflections go here:

31 INTOLERANCE

"Intolerance results from two negative qualities: arrogance and jealousy."

Your own reflections go here:

32 SHOWING UP

"Show up on time and show up ALWAYS.
There lies your success."

Your own reflections go here:

33 DON'T TRY TO PLEASE EVERYONE

"Trying to please everyone leads to quick failure."

Your own reflections go here:

34 TRUE HAPPINESS

"If you are truly happy, either little or massive provision will not make a difference. All provision and blessings would seem too much to bear."

Your own reflections go here:

35 IGNORE THE IGNORANT

"The ignorant ones are so skillful. They will defeat you with their ignorance in any debate or argument. The best medicine for this sickness is to ignore them completely."

Your own reflections go here:

36 ACCEPT CRITICISM

"Criticism, if constructive, is very healthy. Accept it and make it a priority seriously to consider it."

Your own reflections go here:

37 BE PUNCTUAL

"When you tell someone you will meet him/her in 5 minutes, make sure that those 5 minutes comprise only 300 seconds."

Your own reflections go here:

38 BE UPRIGHT AND DO THE RIGHT THING

"Not everything common and acceptable by the masses is right."

Your own reflections go here:

39 FAULTS

"Faults are part of being human. Focus on how to improve yourself in life and those faults will slowly decrease."

Your own reflections go here:

40 PEACE

"Peace requires justice to be achieved."

Your own reflections go here:

41 PRAISE

"Don't exaggeratedly reject people's praise. It may imply that you are seeking more praise."

Your own reflections go here:

42 SILENCE

"Silence is the most eloquent of all speeches; it is better than talking without purpose."

Your own reflections go here:

43 COURAGE

"Courageous people, when faced with the truth, are not afraid of it. They recognize, accept, and live by it."

Your own reflections go here:

44 YOU CAN'T BE CERTAIN
THAT YOU ARE ALWAYS RIGHT

"Be open to the fact that you may be wrong at times."

Your own reflections go here:

45 WHAT TO DO WHEN INSPIRED?

"Inspired people act. Emotional people cry."

Your own reflections go here:

46 INSTANT PLEASURES

"Instant noodles, fast food, 3x1 coffee — these are so quickly made; but, in the end, they leave us unfulfilled. The same applies to instant pleasures. They are so quickly attainable, yet keep us unsatisfied in the end."

Your own reflections go here:

47 DECENT HUMAN BEINGS

"If you wish to test your friends or human beings in general, all you need to do is to wait for when you are hit with adversity."

Your own reflections go here:

48 THE THINGS YOU CANNOT BUY

"You cannot purchase love, peace of mind, or good health; therefore, be grateful when you have them."

Your own reflections go here:

49 REMINDERS

"Don't tire of constant reminders. We tend to forget and sometimes ignore them. Reminders will always be for our own benefit."

Your own reflections go here:

50 ANGER

"Anger is natural. How to demonstrate it is an art."

Your own reflections go here:

51 PAUSING TO REFLECT

"It is always wise to pause, reflect on your thoughts, and give it another shot."

Your own reflections go here:

52 BE CLEAR AND CLARIFY

"When you have something to say, say it clearly. And if you are not understood, clarify further."

Your own reflections go here:

53 BELIEVE IN YOURSELF

"We believe in so many people. We trust them, we follow them, and we do not expect them to be wrong. What is more important, though, is to believe in yourself."

Your own reflections go here:

54 HOW DO YOU UTILIZE YOUR MISTAKES?

"Do not count your mistakes. Instead, use them and bring about something positive from these slip-ups."

Your own reflections go here:

55 WHY DO YOU CARE IF THEY HATE YOU?

"Don't bother yourself with haters. Don't ask yourself, 'Why do they hate me?' They don't really care about you, and you shouldn't care about their opinion, either."

Your own reflections go here:

56 PATIENCE AND SUBMISSIVENESS

"Do not confuse patience with submissiveness. While enduring tough times is required for success and excellence, enduring injustice and oppression is foolishness."

Your own reflections go here:

57 THE CHALLENGE IS WHEN YOU ARE ALONE

"When in public, it is natural that we want to be on our best behavior. The challenge, however, is to monitor yourself when you are alone."

Your own reflections go here:

58 WHO SLEEPS WELL?

"Only honest and sincere people find rest at night. Their days are well spent and they have nothing to fear or hide."

Your own reflections go here:

59 COMPETE

"Don't fear fair competition and don't play dirty games either. Don't deny other people their right to a fair fight."

Your own reflections go here:

60 BEING DIFFERENT

"Be proud of being different. You act, work, talk, and behave differently simply because you are unique. And this is an advantage in itself."

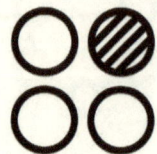

Your own reflections go here:

61 OPEN ENEMIES VS. HYPOCRITES

"An open enemy is honest. He is after you and wants to get rid of you completely. He is truthful about his feelings toward you. A hypocrite is more dangerous. He pretends to be your friend first, and then stabs you in the back."

Your own reflections go here:

62 DON'T NUMB YOUR PAIN

"Address your pain quickly. Numbing your pain increases the chances of desensitization or getting used to that pain or feeling. Don't let pain become part of your life in the sense that it may stop you from moving forward with life."

Your own reflections go here:

63 BEING ALONE WITH YOUR TEARS

"Sometimes it is priceless to sit alone and cry."

Your own reflections go here:

64 MONEY AND MATERIALISM

"Money is great; but, once it controls you,
it becomes destructive."

Your own reflections go here:

65 BEWARE WHERE YOUR GAZE RESTS

"The more you stare, the more you store.
Your gaze could influence your brains and ideas.
So, beware of what you gaze at."

Your own reflections go here:

66 BEING SIMPLE

"Being yourself or being simple can be the hardest thing to do, but it is worth the attempt."

Your own reflections go here:

67 THERE IS ALWAYS THE POSSIBILITY THAT YOU'RE WRONG

"Be absolutely certain that you could be wrong."

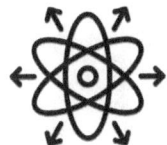

Your own reflections go here:

68 WHAT IS IT YOU SHOULD FEAR?

"You should fear not being able to know what to do in life."

Your own reflections go here:

69 ON HATE THE SIN AND LOVE THE SINNER

"How could anyone abhor the sin but adore the sinner? It is illogical to develop love for one who does something evil."

Your own reflections go here:

70 HONESTY IN TRADE

"Being honest when selling or buying makes you a trusted person in all matters in life."

Your own reflections go here:

71 IF GOODNESS WERE A PRODUCT

"If goodness were a product, even if it is NOT in demand, keep on selling it."

Your own reflections go here:

72 ROUTINE/HABITS

"Creating healthy habits in your life will definitely shape your personality."

Your own reflections go here:

73 SMILE

"Don't worry too much about stretching your jaws or showing your uneven teeth. Smile!"

Your own reflections go here:

74 ILLNESS

"Illness is an inevitable stage that could teach you humility."

Your own reflections go here:

75 WHO WINS?

"History and sports have taught us that winning is not necessarily granted to the strong."

Your own reflections go here:

76 NEW FRIENDS

"Unless a person adds value to you, consider looking for new friends."

Your own reflections go here:

77 DON'T BE STINGY IN SHARING YOUR IDEAS

"Don't worry when sharing great ideas.
You came up with one already. Your creative mind
can come up with a million more."

Your own reflections go here:

78 DON'T RELY SOLELY ON YOUR EMOTIONS

"You don't have to feel good in order to do good."

Your own reflections go here:

79 MANAGING ONE'S SELF

"Unless you learn to manage and control yourself, you will not be able to control your life. And that is called discipline."

Your own reflections go here:

80 PROOF THAT YOU ARE FAITHFUL

"The evidence that you are faithful to a higher being is your level of certainty. And certainty breeds actions."

Your own reflections go here:

81 RELIGION AND MANNERS

"Just because you are religious doesn't mean you are a well-mannered person. In fact, your manners and attitude should result from being religious."

Your own reflections go here:

82 HOW CAN PEOPLE TRUST YOU?

"People can only trust you when your words, actions, and principles are all aligned and consistent."

Your own reflections go here:

83 SEEKING PERFECTION

"You can never be a perfect person in all that you do. In fact, seeking perfection may lead to great disappointment. What you should focus on is doing your best, and that should be sufficient."

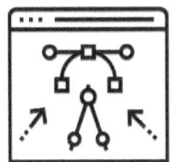

Your own reflections go here:

84 LIVE WITHIN YOUR MEANS

"It is great to be ambitious, but it is greater to be realistic and live within your means. Don't hurt your neck by looking at those above you. Rather, relax it and have a look at those below you."

Your own reflections go here:

85 ADVENTURES

"Be adventurous. You will learn through adventures the art of reflection and insightfulness."

Your own reflections go here:

86 BEAUTIFUL PATIENCE

"Patience could be of two types. Waiting in anger and agony, and waiting with faith and maturity. Things will get easier for those who go for the second type."

Your own reflections go here:

87 GOOD THINGS WILL COME TO AN END

"Be prepared for the heavy moments of life. Loved ones will depart, your best years will pass by, health will deteriorate, and your children's hearts might become hard. All good things will one day come to an end."

Your own reflections go here:

88 APRIL IS NOT A FOOL

"Lies have no colors, and they are not good
on a particular month, either."

Your own reflections go here:

89 THE FOOLISH IS ALWAYS THE LOUDEST

"Often, those who make the most noise are the fools."

Your own reflections go here:

90 HISTORY

"Sometimes, history is intentionally designed, not truthfully told."

Your own reflections go here:

91 TESTING MEN

"Test a man in three cases:
anger, hunger, and poverty."

Your own reflections go here:

92 NODDING

"Do not nod to every sentence in a conversation. In case you have forgotten, nodding indicates approval."

Your own reflections go here:

93 CELIBACY

"Anything that goes against the inborn desires of human beings is bound to fail, including celibacy."

Your own reflections go here:

94 SILENCE VERSUS CONSENT

"Not all silence indicates consent.
Sometimes it is reflective of oppression and fear."

Your own reflections go here:

95 ARE YOU A PEOPLE PLEASER?

"The worst thing you can do to harm yourself is to become a people pleaser."

Your own reflections go here:

96 YOU AND WHAT YOU ARE DOING ARE ENOUGH

"Know wholeheartedly that what you are doing well is worthy and more than enough."

Your own reflections go here:

97 DON'T BE A SLAVE TO AN INHERITED SYSTEM

"We have been conditioned for years to follow a system inherited by our parents and grandparents from their ancestors. On one hand, we should not overlook the values from our past. On the other hand, we shouldn't enslave ourselves to that system if it is no longer relevant to our lives today."

Your own reflections go here:

98 BEING NATURAL

"The fastest way to failure is to be superficial."

Your own reflections go here:

99 ACTIONS BASED ON KNOWLEDGE

"Instead of merely being a human being,
one should first become human 'knowing,' then
right after become human 'doing.'"

Your own reflections go here:

100 GROW UP

"Grow out of being egocentric, always right, and illogical. There are 7 billion people in the world who have something else to offer."

Your own reflections go here:

101 ROLE MODELS

"Growing up without a positive role model is not an excuse for you to live a miserable life. There are people out there in every community who care about you, irrespective of your background. Reach out to them and see the results."

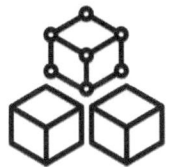

Your own reflections go here:

102 SOMETIMES SHARING IS NOT CARING

"Sharing information concerning your successes won't do you any good, especially if you are sharing the information with people who usually oppose you."

Your own reflections go here:

103 DISRUPT YOUR ROUTINE

"Now and then, disrupt your routine by doing something you have never done before."

Your own reflections go here:

104 CLARITY

"Clarity is to be brave enough to say,
'This is NOT the reason I am here.'"

Your own reflections go here:

How We Should Treat Each Other

105 YOUR MANNERS MATTER

"It is your character that will speak louder than your words. People will ignore your words if your manners are undesirable."

Your own reflections go here:

106 DEALING WITH PEOPLE

"People care little about your vast store of knowledge. They put more value on your showing sincere concern about their condition through kind actions."

Your own reflections go here:

107 FORGETTING VERSUS FORGIVING

"You may never be able to erase the memories of being hurt, but you can choose to forgive those who wronged you."

Your own reflections go here:

108 REJOICE IN THE SUCCESS OF OTHERS

"There is too much already on our plates. Don't stress out when others succeed. Instead, rejoice, wish them well, and give them your full support."

Your own reflections go here:

109 SPEAK AND LISTEN

"Speak all you want to bring your message across, but you must also listen well when others speak."

Your own reflections go here:

110 VALIDATION

"As much as we need validation in life as a way to boost our morale, we need to validate others as well and appreciate their efforts in what they do."

Your own reflections go here:

111 DO NOT ACTIVELY LOOK FOR FAULTS

"You know all about your ugly history.
What's the point of pointing out people's faults?
Hide their faults instead so that your own faults
do not come under focus."

Your own reflections go here:

112 OPINIONS

"Just like how you prefer different types of food, clothes, and so on, other people have their own opinions. Do not impose yours on them."

Your own reflections go here:

113 FRIENDS

"Friends are those who support you,
accept your faults, respond to your call,
and share your moments of happiness and sorrow. When you
find them, don't let go."

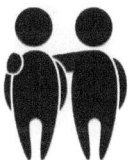

Your own reflections go here:

114 BACKBITING AND GOSSIPING

"Ask yourself what benefit you will gain by mentioning others in their absence with that which you know will hurt them? If you wish this would never happen to you, then respect their absence."

Your own reflections go here:

115 RESPECT TEACHERS AND MENTORS

"How should I speak in front of my teacher? The one who took me all the way to where I am now deserves full respect, and I demonstrate my respect for him by being silent in his presence."

Your own reflections go here:

116 CALL SOMEONE FOR NO REASON

"When are we going to stop calling only because we need favors? When are we going to call just to check on the wellbeing of each other?"

Your own reflections go here:

117 ARGUMENTS

"Don't let arguments lead you to hatred. Learn how to disagree honorably and respectfully."

Your own reflections go here:

118 GOOD GOSSIP

"Speaking well of others in their absence is NOT gossip."

Your own reflections go here:

119 SINCERITY

"What ruins relationships is the lack of sincerity."

Your own reflections go here:

120 WORDS

"Words are like drugs. They can be helpful if used wisely, but we must never misuse them to manipulate others."

Your own reflections go here:

121 SUPPORT

"One of the greatest virtues of all time is to support people when they are at their lowest."

Your own reflections go here:

122 HELPING OTHERS

"Helping others should be seen as a partnership with those you are helping. You are not helping because you are a better person than them. Rather, you are being part of a solution that could positively impact you as well."

Your own reflections go here:

123 SEEKING PERMISSION TO GIVE ADVICE

"Do not impose your opinion or advice on anyone. It's better to seek permission before giving anyone advice or a recommendation."

Your own reflections go here:

124 OUR LAST DAY

"If you think you are superior to anyone, just think of death. We will all end up the same way."

Your own reflections go here:

125 AMAZE YOUR ENEMIES

"Your manners and attitude should amaze your enemies."

Your own reflections go here:

126 LET GO

"I had a dream about an old friend of mine who had conned me out of a certain amount of money. I told him years ago that I will never forgive him. In the dream, we were arguing, and I heard myself telling him the same words, 'I will never forgive you.' When I woke up, I decided to let go of the past and forgive him completely for what he had done."

Your own reflections go here:

127 PEOPLE AREN'T ALL THE SAME

"One of the biggest mistakes people make is thinking that others think the same way."

Your own reflections go here:

128 HOW DID YOU LIVE?

"No one will actually feel how you die. Only YOU will experience that. However, everyone will be interested to know how you lived."

Your own reflections go here:

129 HELPING OTHERS SHOULD REQUIRE NO CONDITION

"Help everyone and anyone. Don't even think of their background or religion."

Your own reflections go here:

130 DON'T LET YOUR CHALLENGES STOP YOU FROM ASSISTING OTHERS

"Set your challenges aside when someone reaches out for help. This is real kindness."

Your own reflections go here:

131 GOSSIP

"Pay attention to what you utter, for gossiping could ruin lives."

Your own reflections go here:

132 HOSPITALITY

"Hospitality only requires a kind heart,
a simple dining table, and a cheerful smile."

Your own reflections go here:

133 BROACH A SUBJECT

"Don't stare emptily into space when you meet someone. Whether you know each other or you are meeting for the first time, be the first to open a useful and beneficial subject."

Your own reflections go here:

134 FEEDING PEOPLE

"One of the noblest acts ever is to distribute food among the needy and hungry. On the top of that, you can also feed them with knowledge, encouragement, validation, and love."

Your own reflections go here:

135 WHAT ARE THEIR NAMES?

"How many times have you forgotten the names of those you've met? Give importance to others. Why don't you learn their names and develop a method not to forget them?"

Your own reflections go here:

136 STORIES & NARRATIVES

"Stories need not TO be always about you. You can use other people's stories, with the intention of validating them and imparting lessons to others."

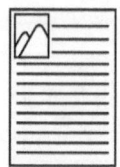

Your own reflections go here:

137 UNEXPECTED VISITS

"Pay unexpected visits to those less fortunate than yourself. Eat with them, spend time with them, and hear their stories."

Your own reflections go here:

138 A NOTE OF HOPE AND LOVE

"Imagine how any person will feel if you unexpectedly pass them a note of love, encouragement, and hope!"

Your own reflections go here:

139 UNDERSTANDING PEOPLE

"It is essential for human beings to make it a priority to understand one another."

Your own reflections go here:

140 SOLVE PROBLEMS

"Make it a point in your life's journey to solve the problems of OTHERS."

Your own reflections go here:

141 UNHEALTHY USE OF EMOTIONS

"Many people use their emotions to control relationships. That is unhealthy."

Your own reflections go here:

142 VALUE OTHERS

"Value everyone you meet by asking them questions, seeking their advice, and asking their opinions."

Your own reflections go here:

143 LOVING OTHERS WITHOUT MEASURE

"You should not love people just because they look good or their character is attractive. You must love them because you have a heart that can accommodate everyone irrespective of their looks and character."

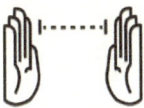

Your own reflections go here:

144 WHAT SHOULD YOU DO WHEN YOU SHOW UP LATE?

"Sometimes you cannot avoid mishaps. But what experiences have taught me is that when you show up late, compensate for the time wasted with a show of excellence."

Your own reflections go here:

145 MISQUOTATION

"Don't you ever misquote anyone
for your own benefit."

Your own reflections go here:

146 GIVE OPPORTUNITIES

"Always do your best to give opportunities to those who have no experience. Otherwise, when will they ever gain experience?"

Your own reflections go here:

Being of Service to Others

147 YOU CAN

"YOU CAN do things that will bring you and others happiness. What are the things you love doing that lets goodness abound? Don't be humble about it. Write them down."

Your own reflections go here:

148 SERVE

"The best thing to do for yourself is to serve others. Adding value to others makes you shine without you even realizing it, because you cannot GET without GIVING."

Your own reflections go here:

149 THE ART OF GIVING

"Most people on earth give charity, but seldom do they give THE BEST of what they have."

Your own reflections go here:

150 WHAT BENEFITS PEOPLE WILL REMAIN

"As for the foam of the sea, it vanishes and casts off. But as for that which benefits the people, it remains on the earth."
–Qur'an 13:11

Your own reflections go here:

151 GIVING

"When you intend to give, don't just give. Rather, give YOUR BEST."

Your own reflections go here:

152 SELFLESSNESS

"Selfless deeds can be defined as favoring other people's needs over your own."

Your own reflections go here:

153 ACTS OF KINDNESS

"Acts of kindness need not TO be complicated. It could be as simple as reading a useful and interesting book to a child."

Your own reflections go here:

154 MONEY

"Money is good only if shared."

Your own reflections go here:

155 MAIDS

"Maids are not made to be enslaved by you. They were made equal to you, so treat them with all kindness, love, and compassion."

Your own reflections go here:

156 BEWARE OF THE MISSING ELEMENT

"Beware of missing compassion when you give charity, devotion when you pray, and sincerity when you offer help."

Your own reflections go here:

157 SPREAD HAPPINESS

"Don't just run after your own happiness. Do your best to make others happy as well."

Your own reflections go here:

158 GIVE SOMETHING UP

"Make it a habit: When you buy something new, give something else you own to someone else in need."

Your own reflections go here:

159 BENEFITS OF MENTORING OTHERS

"Many of my students and clients now contact me every time I announce an event. All of them are ready to assist and make my event a success. This is the benefit of helping someone else; they will also be after your success — a win-win situation."

Your own reflections go here:

Family and Marriage

Family and Marriage

160 EXPRESS YOUR LOVE

"Don't be shy to express your emotions. Many times, we experience mental torture because of not being able to express our love to our loved ones."

Your own reflections go here:

161 FAMILY

"Treasure family members before it is too late. Don't spend all your time on Internet devices in the presence of your loved ones. One day, you would wish to turn back the time to spend a minute with them."

Your own reflections go here:

162 BEING ALONE

"It is OK to be alone sometimes, but make sure never to grow old alone."

Your own reflections go here:

163 MEN AND WOMEN

"Men and women were made so differently.
Men love soccer. Women adore shopping.
It is how we understand each other that will bring about
peace between partners."

Your own reflections go here:

164 LOVE

"When love becomes real, dreams don't matter."

Your own reflections go here:

165 DIVORCE

"Divorce results from two people who married for the wrong reasons."

Your own reflections go here:

166 PARENTS

"There have never been greater people yet to be born than parents. Treasure their presence and serve them until the end."

Your own reflections go here:

167 EXCHANGING SWEET WORDS

"It is all right to express sweet words to those around you. Don't hold your emotions back."

Your own reflections go here:

168 LOYALTY

"Being loyal to people does not end with their demise. Think about how you can serve them even though they are not with us anymore."

Your own reflections go here:

169 CHILDREN

"Your kids may at times not listen to you,
but they will always mimic you. So, be the best of examples
to them."

Your own reflections go here:

170 JOY IN MARRIAGE

"There's no joy in being alone. That's why I love the institution of marriage."

Your own reflections go here:

171 SAYING I LOVE YOU

"Tell your loved ones you are truly in love with them. Tell them that every day."

Your own reflections go here:

172 PERFECT SPOUSE

"There is no perfect spouse. If you are seeking one, the best thing to do is to first try to be one yourself."

Your own reflections go here:

173 ACCEPT REALITIES

"Teach your children to accept realities. It is often difficult for us to bear the heaviness of truth, but truth will remain the best to live by."

Your own reflections go here:

174 HOW DOES HE TREAT HIS MOTHER?

"To the ladies, I always say, marry the one who treats his mother like a queen."

Your own reflections go here:

175 AFFECTION

"As much as you love to receive affection,
learn to give it."

Your own reflections go here:

176 FAMILY MEMBERS OF THE PAST

"Remember your family members who passed away, relate their stories to your children, and treasure the golden memories."

Your own reflections go here:

177 MOST PAINFUL MOMENT

"When I think that one day I will depart from this world and leave behind my family members, my children, and loved ones, it makes me feel so scared and concerned. But it is a reality. Have hope in the legacy you will leave behind to your loved ones and fear will cease to exist."

Your own reflections go here:

178 DON'T HARM OTHERS BY HARMING YOURSELF

"Never harm yourself, physically or emotionally. If you ever stop caring about yourself, remember that you mean the world to some people out there."

Your own reflections go here:

179 YOUR WIVES

"To the men I say, 'Be gentle to your wives, or else you don't deserve to be called men.'"

Your own reflections go here:

180 YOUR HUSBANDS

"To the women I say, 'Don't think with a man's brain. You won't like it."

Your own reflections go here:

181 HOME IS HOME

"Home is meant to be a place where peace of mind is achieved. Now, how can you have peace of mind if you are always absent from home?"

Your own reflections go here:

182 ARE YOU LOVED AT HOME?

"It doesn't matter if the entire world is celebrating how cheerful, kind, and well-mannered you are. If your family members have a different view, then you've lost all credibility."

Your own reflections go here:

183 HEALTHY ATTACHMENTS

"To always feel the need to be with those you love is the definition of a healthy relationship."

Your own reflections go here:

184 LIVING WITH IN-LAWS

"To me, the greatest mistake any couple could make is to live with their parents after their marriage."

Your own reflections go here:

185 FAMILY MEMBERS WORKING FOR THE SAME INSTITUTION

"Two competent family members working for the same institution makes it an incompetent workplace."

Your own reflections go here:

186 BEFRIEND YOUR KIDS

"A friend would let go of your mistakes and faults. Treat your kids like how you would treat your friends. In other words, befriend your kids."

Your own reflections go here:

187 ENCOURAGE YOUR CHILDREN

"Whatever talent they have, encourage your kids and invest in what they love. Just because you do not favor that particular talent does not give you the right to shut them off."

Your own reflections go here:

Success and Greatness

188 RECIPE FOR SUCCESS

"The ingredients for success are (1) willingness,
(2) hard work, (3) enjoying the challenges along the way, (4) repeating what works well, and
(5) not being foolish by duplicating mistakes."

Your own reflections go here:

189 FEAR NO MORE

"Don't fear taking action. It is OK and expected to fail sometimes in life, but the taste of success will never be forgotten."

Your own reflections go here:

190 SMALL DEEDS, GREAT SUCCESS

"Keep on escalating to reach the sky, one mile at a time. No rush and no competition. What matters is to get where you want to be."

Your own reflections go here:

191 EVERYTHING IS YOUR RESPONSIBILITY

"Blame no one for failure. Everything you do is YOURS and depends on YOU alone, so take responsibility for your own actions."

Your own reflections go here:

192 ASK YOURSELF

"Whenever you see successful people, ask yourself, 'Why not me as well? Why is it not my time yet?' Watch what they do, learn from them, and then supersede them all."

Your own reflections go here:

193 DON'T RELY ON YOUR SUCCESS

"One of the gravest errors is to rely too much on what you have already achieved."

Your own reflections go here:

194 FOCUS

"It is what you focus on that will truly be accomplished. What you spend most of the time thinking of and working on is what will be attained."

Your own reflections go here:

195 THE JOURNEY OF LIFE

"Our lives are measured by seconds, minutes, hours, days, and years. So, make every step count.
Take one step at a time to achieve greatness. Mediocrity is not an option."

Your own reflections go here:

196 YOU ALONE ARE NOT GOOD ENOUGH

"We need each other to excel in all matters. Greatness cannot be achieved by one person working alone. You'll need other people's help on the long road to success."

Your own reflections go here:

197 MAKING A DIFFERENCE

"We know of people throughout history who created differences in their lives and the world at large. You can leave a similar legacy. They are not any better than YOU."

Your own reflections go here:

198 GOALS

"If you don't have targets to achieve, then you are going NOWHERE."

Your own reflections go here:

199 TWO SUCCESS KEYS

"Without discipline and consistency, do not expect progress and success."

Your own reflections go here:

200 MINDSET

"Having the right mindset is everything. If you really believe you can achieve what you dream of and do the necessary action, it is a done deal."

Your own reflections go here:

201 FULFILLING DREAMS

"Dreams aren't real, unless you wake up and make them happen."

Your own reflections go here:

202 LEAVE A LEGACY AND SOME MEMORIES

"My father didn't leave treasures behind, but he left a greater legacy: values and great memories."

Your own reflections go here:

203 ACCEPT REALITY

"If things didn't go your way, adjust to the situation and find a different way that may not necessarily be YOUR WAY."

Your own reflections go here:

204 LITTLE BY LITTLE

"Do not be in a hurry to achieve your goals. Success happens one little step at a time."

Your own reflections go here:

205 ADJUSTMENT & ADAPTABILITY

"Adjustment and adaptability are the solutions needed along the journey of success."

Your own reflections go here:

206 BEING BUSY

"Being busy doing things you are not passionate about is a waste of time."

Your own reflections go here:

207 DO NOT SURRENDER TO IDLENESS

"Success comes to those who utilize their spare time and do not lie around doing nothing."

Your own reflections go here:

208 PEOPLE WHO MATTER

"Don't be excited when people cheer for you when you succeed. What you truly need are those who would surround you when you fail."

Your own reflections go here:

209 AMBITION

"Being ambitious is not a problem. But, in the pursuit of what you wish to achieve, always appreciate and be grateful for what you already have."

Your own reflections go here:

210 REMEMBER THOSE WHO HELPED YOU

"When you succeed in life, remember that you did not do it on your own. Find those who've helped you and make them part of your success."

Your own reflections go here:

211 PRESSURE

"It is with pressure that one could burst with success."

Your own reflections go here:

212 THE TWO CS OF SUCCESS

"Remember, you will always have a CHOICE, and you will always be able to CHANGE, if you want to."

Your own reflections go here:

213 BE APPROACHABLE

"No matter how far you've come, remain down-to-earth and be approachable."

Your own reflections go here:

214 SUCCESSFUL IDEAS

"All successful ideas were rejected in the beginning."

Your own reflections go here:

215 UPHILL BATTLES

"Only when you are at the top can you truly enjoy the view. Ascending is hard, but the view from the top is worth the effort."

Your own reflections go here:

216 IDENTIFY YOUR STRENGTHS

"To hit your goals and reach the maximum achievement for which you hope, you must identify your strengths and weaknesses. Otherwise, there will be no room to improve."

Your own reflections go here:

217 ARCHERY

"In archery, they teach us that to hit the target, aim a bit above it. Aim high and you will get what you want."

Your own reflections go here:

Taking Action

218 DREAM IT, ACT IT

"Without action you will go nowhere.
DREAM all you want, but making your dreams come true requires action."

Your own reflections go here:

219 OUTPERFORM YOURSELF

"Unless you outperform yourself and shine to the best of your ability, the changes you are hoping to see in your life may never see the light."

Your own reflections go here:

220 DUE DATES

"Don't wait for the due dates to start on your tasks. Just DO them."

Your own reflections go here:

221 DON'T RELY ON MOTIVATION

"Don't let motivation be the primary force in your life. Rather, act anyway whether or not you are motivated. Actions breed results."

Your own reflections go here:

222 INCREASE YOUR ENERGY

"If there's no increase in your energy and success, there will be a decrease. It is one or the other. Decide where you want to be."

Your own reflections go here:

223 CHANGE WILL HAPPEN

"With or without you, changes are inevitable. The world will keep going on, so you better be part of the positive changes that WILL happen."

Your own reflections go here:

224 KEEP THE EFFORT ON

"What people want to see from you is pursuit and effort. Do what you can. Results will follow."

Your own reflections go here:

225 INTENTION WITHOUT ACTION IS NOT GOOD ENOUGH

"Intent to do good is good, but never good enough unless good actions accompany it."

Your own reflections go here:

226 DAY IN AND DAY OUT

"Do yourself a favor and be consistent in what you do. Working day in and day out is what completes any mission."

Your own reflections go here:

227 ENVIRONMENT

"If your surroundings and environment are not conducive enough to achieve goodness and excellence, the answer is simple. CHANGE THEM."

Your own reflections go here:

228 TODAY ONLY POLICY

"You cannot bring back the past. Nobody can guarantee what tomorrow brings. All you have is today to create the changes you want to see in this world."

Your own reflections go here:

229 DON'T DEMAND, WORK HARD

"You can choose to demand promotions,
extra rewards and so on. But you can gain all of that without
demanding, if you just work hard and
excel in what you do."

Your own reflections go here:

230 PREPARATION

"Preparation breeds confidence. Always be ready."

Your own reflections go here:

231 PROCRASTINATION

"The shortest way to failure is delaying what you need to do TODAY."

Your own reflections go here:

232 NOTHING HAPPENS BY CHANCE

"It is your choices in life that make a difference. Nothing is by chance."

Your own reflections go here:

233 DO NOT LOOK BACK

"To enjoy what lies ahead, keep moving forward and never look back."

Your own reflections go here:

234 FOCUS ON WHAT YOU CAN CONTROL

"The things you cannot control will never help you. Direct your entire focus on what you CAN control, and that's where you can start moving forward."

Your own reflections go here:

235 TAKE OFF

"Taking off is the hardest in any journey,
but once in the air, you can set the remainder
of the trip on auto-pilot."

Your own reflections go here:

236 7 WORDS

"'Say yes, and then work out how' are the 7 most important words I've learned in recent years. They've directed me to the importance of taking action and learning at the same time instead of waiting for miracles to happen."

Your own reflections go here:

237 TRY VERSUS DO

"Words impact our behaviors. This is a fact. So, instead of saying 'I will try my best,' replace it with, 'I will DO my best,' and see what happens."

Your own reflections go here:

238 WASTING LIFE

"Don't waste your life on preparation. Learn to take action by making quick decisions based on knowledge, mentorship, and, above all, faith. Don't wait too long to get started; it is a waste of life."

Your own reflections go here:

239 IDEAS

"There's no value in an idea without putting it to action."

Your own reflections go here:

240 THE POOL OF FEAR

"If you wish to swim, do not paralyze yourself.
Jump into the pool and figure out how to float. Address fear
in the same way."

Your own reflections go here:

241 DO NOT WAIT FOR THE 'RIGHT' TIME

"Doing the right thing need not wait for a long time to be decided. Just go for it once you realize it is right."

Your own reflections go here:

242 YOU DON'T HAVE TIME?

"If you say, 'I don't have time' to do what you know is essential, I will simply not believe you."

Your own reflections go here:

243 START AT ANY STAGE

"You don't have to wait until you become an expert in order for you to do something great. All you need to do is to start doing something."

Your own reflections go here:

244 BAD NEWS VERSUS GOOD NEWS

"The bad news is that life is too short. The good news is that you are still alive, so don't waste your life."

Your own reflections go here:

245 UNTIL WHEN YOU WILL KEEP PUTTING OFF STUFF YOU WISH TO EXECUTE?

"What you wish to see tomorrow has to be executed today, so bring to light that which you've been putting off for years."

Your own reflections go here:

246 DON'T MAKE LIFE SHORTER

"As is often said, life is too short. No time should be wasted making it even shorter."

Your own reflections go here:

247 DAILY ROUTINE

"If you do not have a daily agenda on which to work, then you are wasting a lot of time."

Your own reflections go here:

Focus, Passion and Perseverance

248 YOUR HEART

"Pour your heart into what YOU CAN DO. Let your heart be the compass that will direct you, and let your hands be the tools to get things done."

Your own reflections go here:

249 DREAM IT

"All great and successful people have seen their dreams come true because they took that critical first step and dreamt big."

Your own reflections go here:

250 ACHIEVE MORE

"When you achieve something great, acknowledge that it was no easy feat, but do not rest on your laurels. Move forward, faster than ever, and achieve more."

Your own reflections go here:

251 TAKING RISKS

"Risk always accompanies opportunity.
Taking on some risk in life is not gambling if
the steps taken are not thoughtless.
Embrace uncertainty in matters you love the most."

Your own reflections go here:

252 DO NOT LET YOURSELF BE INTERRUPTED

"You cannot do everything in life all at once.
Do not let things that you cannot do interrupt you. Focus on what you CAN do and let others do their own thing."

Your own reflections go here:

253 PASSION

"Being passionate about what you do is great. Demonstrating your passion is even greater."

Your own reflections go here:

254 OUTCOME

"Outcome is determined by faith, dedication, willingness, hard work, and teamwork."

Your own reflections go here:

255 FINISH WHAT YOU HAVE STARTED

"Do not give up easily. Often, we get excited about something and then later lose motivation. Learn to finish what you have started. An injured athlete will keep running even though he knows he has lost the race, because what matters is not winning, but commitment to completion."

Your own reflections go here:

256 SPECIAL SKILLS

"Don't rely on your special skills or talent only. Unless you exert effort with planning and preparation, your talents may betray you."

Your own reflections go here:

257 WANT TO BE YOUNGER AGAIN?

"If you wish to be young again, be productive."

Your own reflections go here:

258 ONE DROP AT A TIME COMPLETES AN ENTIRE OCEAN

"The 365 quotes of this book were compiled one day at a time. The number seems too big to fathom, yet the task has been completed. The same applies with every other task, one little bit at a time."

Your own reflections go here:

259 QUESTIONS TO ASK YOURSELF BEFORE MAKING A POSITIVE CHANGE

"Am I willing to change? Am I committed to change? Will I bear the temporary pain associated with making a change?"

Your own reflections go here:

260 BEING CONSISTENT

"It is difficult to remain consistent all the time.
This is a truth that every individual must realize.
We just have to do our best to do what we can to improve ourselves when we err."

Your own reflections go here:

261 WORK FROM YOUR HEART

"Don't wait to be told what you should or shouldn't do at work. Just work sincerely from your heart."

Your own reflections go here:

262 DON'T WORRY ABOUT TAKING CREDIT

"Give credit away. You don't need recognition. You just need to get the job done."

Your own reflections go here:

263 MOMENTUM

"You can only keep your momentum if you keep pushing your limits repeatedly. Once you relax to celebrate, the momentum is gone."

Your own reflections go here:

264 BE A BEGINNER

"Always remain in your student hat,
ready to learn more."

Your own reflections go here:

265 DON'T REMAIN THE SAME

"Always be on a nonstop journey of improvement."

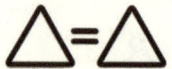

Your own reflections go here:

266 THE SPIRIT OF WORK

"Learn to do simple or hard work with the same spirit."

Your own reflections go here:

267 THE BEES & THE ANTS

"My favorite insects are the bees and the ants. They work tirelessly until their last breath."

Your own reflections go here:

268 NEW YEAR'S RESOLUTIONS

"A New Year's resolution should run for 12 months and followed through for life, not for 2 weeks."

Your own reflections go here:

Overcoming Adversity

Overcoming Adversity

269 THE JOURNEY WILL NOT BE EASY

"Don't let every difficulty encountered stop you. Instead, embrace the difficulties in life and create opportunities to cope with them."

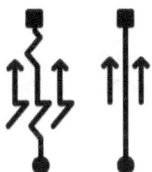

Your own reflections go here:

270 NOTHING IS ROUGH ALL THE WAY

"A rough patch of road does not suggest a bumpy journey all the way. Smooth road may be just up ahead."

Your own reflections go here:

271 QUICK FIXES DO NOT ACTUALLY FIX

"We often make mistakes and that is okay. But opting for shortcuts may take you even longer to fix your mistakes in the long run. Do not settle and never rely on quick fixes."

Your own reflections go here:

272 CONVERT THE NEGATIVE INTO POSITIVE

"It is how you perceive situations that makes all the difference in the world. Your attitude could see the problem as an opportunity or as an unsolvable obstacle."

Your own reflections go here:

273 U-TURNS

"U-TURNs exist for a reason. Don't hesitate to turn back when things go wrong."

Your own reflections go here:

274 OBSTACLES

"When you face obstacles in life, you will always have three options to deal with them: (1) Sit and cry over your condition, (2) blame everyone and the day that brought you to this destination, or (3) go around the obstacles and proceed to the intended destination."

Your own reflections go here:

275 LIFE IS TOUGH

"Life can be difficult. Be prepared to get hurt,
but also be willing to be healed."

Your own reflections go here:

276 ADVERSITY

"Hardship and calamity may appear as something bad from our perspective. But for others, they may be considered as turning points that make one grow stronger."

Your own reflections go here:

277 IMPOSSIBLE IS NOT A WORD

"Delete the word impossible from your vocabulary in order for you to achieve success. Make this declaration loud and clear: Impossible is NOT A WORD."

Your own reflections go here:

278 HAPPINESS AND PAIN

"Many of us do not realize that in search of our happiness and convenience, we often escape from the pain and discomfort we need to experience. Unless you address these moments of pain, you won't be able to find true happiness."

Your own reflections go here:

279 PANIC

"Panic is the easiest way to worsen any situation."

Your own reflections go here:

280 DO NOT AVOID CONFRONTATIONS

"Words impact our actions, attitudes, and decisions. If you fear to 'confront' people, then why don't you 'meet' them to 'clarify' your position and 'rectify' any issue that caused the misunderstanding?"

Your own reflections go here:

281 PAINFUL EXPERIENCES

"Painful experiences could be
the greatest lessons in life."

Your own reflections go here:

282 ACCEPTANCE AND RESOLVING

"When you face a fact, after evaluating all evidence, accept it. When you face a problem, after understanding the cause, solve it."

Your own reflections go here:

283 NICK VUJICIC

"Nick Vujicic has no limbs, but his will and determination keep moving him forward and up."

Your own reflections go here:

284 WHEN THE ROAD IS THORNY

"When the road is rough and thorny, don't rush forward.
Make your choice wisely. Walk cautiously,
stand still, or turn back."

Your own reflections go here:

285 POSITIVITY NOT EXPERIENCED 24/7

"We may not experience positivity every single day of the year. Sometimes we feel down, tired, and sick. But so long as we trust ourselves to turn the negative into positive, then don't worry about these annoying moments."

Your own reflections go here:

286 MY INTERVIEW WITH AN ATHLETE

"He told me that pain during training wasn't in his dictionary. For him, pain was part of the package that led him to the ultimate pleasure — victory and championship."

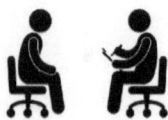

Your own reflections go here:

287 IGNORE YOUR ENEMIES

"Your enemies could never be killed with love. Only by pretending they don't exist can you destroy them."

Your own reflections go here:

On Leadership

288 EXCEPTIONAL LEADERS

"Great leaders live and die for two things: their mission and their people."

Your own reflections go here:

289 DEMOCRACY

"Democracy means the majority would win anyway without considering the opinion of the minority."

Your own reflections go here:

290 GOOD QUESTIONS

"Good leaders should ask great questions at the appropriate time and place. Good questions make us think well, and this is what brings about transformation."

Your own reflections go here:

291 PUBLIC SPEAKING

"The one skill that you should learn before anything else is public speaking. You will surely need it in almost every situation in life."

Your own reflections go here:

292 INTERNATIONAL EVENTS

"International speaking engagements have taught me that I should focus more on my locality."

Your own reflections go here:

293 YOUR ATTITUDE AND YOUR TEAM

"If you are leading a team, your positive attitude matters much. Otherwise, you may influence them negatively."

Your own reflections go here:

294 VISION SHARING

"The more you share your vision with others, the more members will join you to make it a reality."

Your own reflections go here:

295 COMPETENCY

"If you are competent in what you do, then be an example and require it from everyone in your circle."

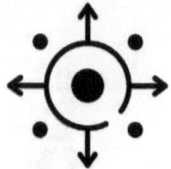

Your own reflections go here:

296 INVEST IN OTHERS

"To mentor others in order for them to shine and become leaders of the future is the hallmark of being a great leader."

Your own reflections go here:

297 WHEN THINGS GO WRONG

"Go for it. Take responsibility when things go wrong. This is a sign of an honorable leader."

Your own reflections go here:

298 DELEGATE

"When you are overwhelmed with work, delegate tasks to others, but never run away from responsibility."

Your own reflections go here:

299 COPING WITH DIFFERENT MINDS

"You are successful only when you can work with people of different mindsets."

Your own reflections go here:

300 TEAMWORK

"The term TEAMWORK is self-explanatory. You will need MORE THAN ONE PERSON (TEAM) to get the WORK done."

Your own reflections go here:

301 LEADERSHIP QUALITY

"All leaders were once great followers. Unless you obey today, you won't be able to lead tomorrow."

Your own reflections go here:

On Addiction

302 WHAT IS ADDICTION?

"When you prioritize actions that may lead you (knowingly) to destructive consequences, this is addiction."

Your own reflections go here:

303 ADDICTIONS

"Addictions are like battles. They are not fought only once. You may need to return to the battlefield more than once to clean your mess. So, keep on fighting."

Your own reflections go here:

304 HABITS

"Habits, good or bad, are formed through continuous repetition."

Your own reflections go here:

305 PORN ADDICTION AWARENESS

"We must raise awareness about porn addiction. It is not a matter of life and death. It is scarier than that."

Your own reflections go here:

306 RELAPSES

"Addicts may relapse throughout their journey of recovery. Consider them as slips. You experience them. Then stand up again and proceed with the route."

Your own reflections go here:

307 PORN INDUSTRY

"The multi-billion-dollar industry of pornography has made intimacy between spouses irrelevant, boring, and unattractive. Since you have access to millions of sexy models of all sizes and shapes, why would you care to even look at your spouse?"

Your own reflections go here:

308 LONELINESS

"The first step toward recovery from any addiction is not to be alone ever again."

Your own reflections go here:

309 QUIT THE HABITS THAT ARE HOLDING YOU BACK

"All habits that are holding you back from excelling in life should be broken. Though I hate the word SHOULD, this is an exception."

Your own reflections go here:

310 BEWARE OF ALL ADDICTIONS

"You could become addicted to absolutely anything — procrastination, laziness, useless TV shows, social media, pornography, etc. If you have a problem, you know what to do: Seek help and do something else beneficial."

Your own reflections go here:

311 THE PAIN OF ADDICTION

"Every addict knows addiction results in nothing but pain, but few are aware that the beginning of addiction comes from an unspoken emotional pain."

Your own reflections go here:

Knowledge and Wisdom

312 MATURING

"The older you get, the more you realize how many errors you made when you were young. Don't regret the mistakes. Rather, keep on doing right in the remaining days of your life."

Your own reflections go here:

313 BOOKS

"Books are the best investment you could ever make in your life. It is like hiring the greatest minds in the world for the cheapest price ever."

Your own reflections go here:

314 ASK

"Be curious and don't worry if people may get annoyed when you ask too many questions. Questioning leads to solutions."

Your own reflections go here:

315 MASTER WHAT YOU KNOW

"Gather knowledge when you can. Then get in control of what you know by sharing it."

Your own reflections go here:

316 BOOKS, AGAIN

"I have not yet found any book to be entirely boring or bad. Every book I've read has something beneficial in it."

Your own reflections go here:

317 KNOWLEDGE VERSUS WISDOM

"One can easily gather knowledge; but, to attain wisdom, you will have to live and act upon your knowledge. Don't just be a knowledge gatherer."

Your own reflections go here:

318 YOUR STORY MATTERS

"There's always wisdom to be gleaned from what happened to you in the past. Imagine how many lives you can positively impact by sharing your story."

Your own reflections go here:

319 EDUCATION

"Invest in education and learning. The alternative is ignorance and misguidance."

Your own reflections go here:

320 DOUBTS

"It is OK to have doubts, but seek answers quickly before you get used to being in that state forever."

Your own reflections go here:

321 MODERN-DAY SCHOOLING

"Never think that schools provide education. The education system aims to make you robots, not intellectual and creative."

Your own reflections go here:

322 MY COLLECTION OF BOOKS

"I've commanded my family members never to sell or give away my collection of books after my demise. This is part of my last will and testament."

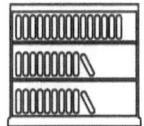

Your own reflections go here:

323 LEARN AND TEACH

"Do not keep knowledge to yourself. As much as you love to learn, teach."

Your own reflections go here:

324 APPLY WHAT'S IN THE BOOKS

"A great book on the shelf wouldn't do you any favor unless you read it. Reading a great book wouldn't do you any good unless you apply what's in it."

Your own reflections go here:

325 LOSING IS A LEARNING JOURNEY

"Do not grieve when you lose things in life. Be certain that with every loss is a learning experience that will add value to you in life."

Your own reflections go here:

326 KNOWLEDGE ISN'T ALWAYS POWER

"Knowledge isn't power; implementing knowledge is."

Your own reflections go here:

327 SEIZE ALL OPPORTUNITIES

"Don't pass on any opportunity that could take you up to a whole different level, especially all learning opportunities."

Your own reflections go here:

Reflecting on Everyday Life

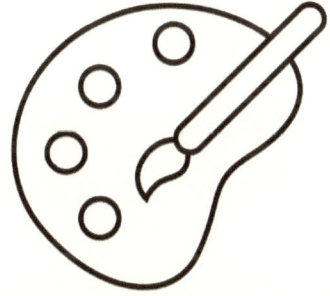

328 DOGS

"Dogs never cease to amaze me. Their loyalty, love, and absolute dedication to their masters are things that human beings should definitely practice."

Your own reflections go here:

329 FACEBOOK "FRIENDS"

"Ask yourself, how many REAL friends are there on Facebook? What is even more important, what is your definition of a true friend?"

Your own reflections go here:

330 SUNSET

"The sunset is the ultimate example that nothing remains static."

Your own reflections go here:

331 I AM THE GREATEST

"Perhaps Muhammad Ali was egocentric and overconfident, but what was apparent to all was that he knew he was too good to be ignored."

Your own reflections go here:

332 WE ARE INCREDIBLE CREATURES

"The whole universe was subjugated for our benefit. We fly heavyweight aircraft, surf the water, train wild beasts. We build amazing infrastructure. We flip ourselves in the air, and we jump off planes. How could we then fail in our work? That would be through our fault alone."

Your own reflections go here:

333 THE IRONY OF LIFE

"Life is full of ironies. One of them is that you will sometimes miss out on what you want the most."

Your own reflections go here:

334 LEAVE YOUR PHONES

"Do not get too attached to your Internet devices, especially when someone is talking to you. You cannot focus on the conversation while staring at something else that is completely distracting."

Your own reflections go here:

335 FOR EVERY LOCATION, A PARTICULAR BEHAVIOR

"At the dining table, eat. In the bedroom, sleep. In a classroom, focus. On the toilet, finish your business. Don't use your cell phones in the above-mentioned locations."

Your own reflections go here:

336 FACEBOOK COMMENTS

"Only those who have nothing to do will worry about people's comments on Facebook."

Your own reflections go here:

337 SOCCER/FOOTBALL

"I love football, though I am not sure why a ball kicked around by 22 players can mesmerize millions of people around the globe!"

Your own reflections go here:

338 TELEGRAPHS

"Telegraphs of the past (not telegrams) were costly, short, and very thoughtful. Today, most WhatsApp shared messages are long, free, but usually nonsensical."

Your own reflections go here:

339 YOUR WORDS ARE YOUR LIFE

"Do not dissociate your teachings from your life. What you utter should be lived."

Your own reflections go here:

340 UNREASONABLE FOLKS

"Unreasonable people are called as such because no sane person can reason with them."

Your own reflections go here:

341 PROPAGANDA

"A lot of media outlets are after creating propaganda and juicy stories. They are not really after reporting the truth."

Your own reflections go here:

342 LEAVING IS PAINFUL

"Sometimes in life, you will have no option but to leave behind something dear to your heart. It is painful, but sometimes necessary."

Your own reflections go here:

343 ACTING

"I have never understood why actors and actresses, who are not married or in relationships, would allow each other to hug and kiss and simulate sex scenes! Don't they have real spouses or partners?"

Your own reflections go here:

344 JOURNALISTS

"Journalists, if honest, would never allow lies to be published."

Your own reflections go here:

345 IRRESPONSIBLE MEDIA CONTENT

"Over-sexualized media content, including children's movies, is destroying our kids."

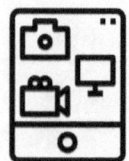

Your own reflections go here:

346 WE DIE, YET WE HAVE A CHANCE TO LEAVE A LEGACY

"We are all going to die, but few will be remembered forever after their departure."

Your own reflections go here:

347 IN BUSINESS

"In business, try to point out the faults of your products to your buyer. They may not buy that particular product; but, in the future, they will consider no one else but you as a business partner."

Your own reflections go here:

348 IGNORANCE OF THE LAW

"I do agree that ignorance of the law is no excuse for breaking it, but how can it be said that the ignorant are intentionally breaking the law?"

Your own reflections go here:

349 FISHING AND TRAFFIC JAMS

"Fishing, as well as the traffic jams in Southeast Asia and the Middle East, teaches patience."

Your own reflections go here:

350 TEACHING ELDERS

"It is nearly impossible to teach elders like our parents or grannies. We must, however, make them discover the truth of what we intend to teach them without hurting their feelings."

Your own reflections go here:

351 MONDAYS

"I find it very strange that most people hate Mondays when it is just the first day of the week! How do they spend the rest of the week then?"

Your own reflections go here:

352 SMILE AT PEOPLE

"Isn't it strange that we see people walking around smiling at their phones; but, once they raise their heads, their smiles are gone?"

Your own reflections go here:

353 MAKEUP

"The absence of wearing makeup makes people question if the person is sick. This is the impact of artificial products. You are beautiful the way you were originally made. Don't ruin that."

Your own reflections go here:

354 RUNNING AFTER DISCOUNTS

"We get excited when we see a sign that says '30% off,' but have we thought about whether we could afford the other 70% at all?"

Your own reflections go here:

355 SPEAKERPHONE

"Before putting anyone on speakerphone, seek their permission."

Your own reflections go here:

356 FIRST SIGHT NOT ALWAYS RIGHT

"How many times have you told a friend, 'When I first met you, I hated you,' then you ended up being best friends?"

Your own reflections go here:

357 LOSING WEIGHT AND OTHER THINGS

"As much as we love to lose weight and be in better shape, we should also aim to lose hatred, jealousy, animosity, carelessness, and greed."

Your own reflections go here:

358 BACKSEAT DRIVERS

"Don't be shy to silence them throughout the journey; because, if you don't, backseat drivers could cause your next disastrous accident."

Your own reflections go here:

359 MEETINGS

"I never enjoyed meetings in my olden days. They were held to point fingers at employees' mistakes. They were the most painful moments of my job."

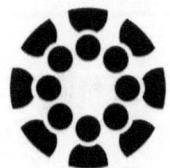

Your own reflections go here:

360 TV SERIES

"My friend just told me she has watched 7 seasons, 114 episodes of a TV series she loves. Now you have a good example of what time wasting is."

Your own reflections go here:

361 INDIAN MOVIES

"I love the Indian people, but I don't like their movies. Their imagination in violent scenes is so dramatic it could lead you to real violence. Stay away from watching them."

Your own reflections go here:

362 BEING MESSY

"Some people are so disorganized even though all they do in life is play video games or lie down in bed."

Your own reflections go here:

363 FAVORITE PART OF YOUR JOB

"If your favorite part of your job is to go home, then you should find another job."

Your own reflections go here:

364 SHOPAHOLICS

"It always amazes me when people complain about money all the time yet go crazy buying stuff online and in shopping centers."

Your own reflections go here:

365 VARIETY

"Life would be a bore without a variety of languages, people, and cultures."

Your own reflections go here:

ACKNOWLEDGEMENTS

The work of BetterMe: 365 Ways To Transform Your Everyday Life could've never come to light without the assistance and professional help of the following amazing people:

J.P. Bautista – Editor of the 365 quotes and the one who painstakingly have grouped the quotes into categories in such an amazing and professional manner.

Ebony Harper – Creative designer of the book cover who will never settle until she brings out the best work possible and suitable for the project.

Mufti Ismail Menk – a dear and a real friend of mine who, despite his busy schedule, would never tire of responding to my constant messages and inquiries. Thanks for making yourself always available, not only to your friends, but to the public as well.

My family, wife and children – Thanks for always being patient when I am not in a good shape. Your patience and support can never be rewarded enough.

AFTERWORD

So I am already in the planning stage of producing part two of BetterMe – The application Method – which is going to be based on your reflections of the 365 ways/quotes recorded in this book. You don't have to reflect on all the quotes; just focus on whatever is relevant to you, and that would be more than sufficient.

So here's the deal. Read the book, jot down your reflections in the spaces provided, take clear pictures of what you wrote (please avoid doctors' handwriting) and share them with me. It is that simple. Then in a couple of months or so, BetterMe PART II will include your reflections and the application part, which will be suggested.

So all the balls now are in your court.

Waiting to read your reflections to take the BetterMe into the next level.

Wael Ibrahim
wael@wael-ibrahim.com

US$3.90 ONLY
In PDF

For the holders of this book ONLY
Email us a screen shot of your post
on your social media platforms while:
1. Holding the #BetterMe book
2. Use the hashtag #BetterMe
3. Tag Wael Ibrahim
And the above offer is yours :)

wael@wael-ibrahim.com

SPEAKING ENGAGEMENTS

Inspirational Talks
Training
Workshops
Seminars
Courses
Certification programs

Contact wael@wael-ibrahim.com
for more details

BETTER Me
COURSE

Becoming #BetterYOU on a deeper level

Apply today and enjoy 50% discount and the entire value of the #BetterMe in-depth course.

Call or email: +61 414 919 806
wael@wael-ibrahim.com

#SAVEHER

2 DAYS TRAINING FOR 50 LADIES ONLY

VERY LIMITED SPOTS

Learn how to save her from the destructive addiction of our age.

PORNOGRAPHY

CALL OR EMAIL FOR DETAILS

Wael@wael-ibrahim.com
+61414919806

www.ingramcontent.com/pod-product-compliance
Lightning Source LLC
Chambersburg PA
CBHW031054080526
44587CB00011B/679